I0415570

Ferenc Margitics Ph.D.

THE SPIRITUAL CONSCIOUSNESS SCALE
handbook

Cover: Pexels, http://bit.ly/2ZlgXsn

Authored by: Ferenc Margitics PhD
(margitics.ferenc@nye.hu)
Published by: Ervin K. Kery
(editor@ kery.org)

www.consciousnessbooks.cf

Preface

In the past fifteen or twenty years, there has been considerable research into the effects of religion and spirituality on people's physical and mental health.

Today, the polarization of two concepts is observable: religion represents everything that comes from the outside, it is formal and institutional, whereas spirituality represents everything that is subjective, personal, emotional, comes from the inside and is not systematic.

Eckhart Tolle draws our attention to another approach to spirituality. In his opinion, our present consciousness opens up the gate to spirituality. The individual must experience the present moment, while the alertness of his/her consciousness enables the person to view his or her own thoughts, emotions and reactions triggered by the stimuli of the environment.

The Presence thus created (conscious alertness) brings about the sense of tranquility and internal peace. The sustained conscious attention launches the spiritual process of transubstatiation that leads the individual to a Spiritual Consciousness, new perspective and new ways of observing. This process, by transforming the consciousness of the person, changes the entire personality of the individual.

The author makes an effort to approach this process with the means of scientific research. Following the teachings of Eckhart Tolle, the author created the Spiritual Consciousness Scale (SCS) and carried out its statistical analysis. The purpose has been developing a new measuring instrument for the recognition of spiritual consciousness.

Psychometric Characteristics of the Spiritual Consciousness Scale

1. Introduction

1.1. Religion and Spirituality

The history of research into the psychology religion and spirituality is relatively brief, as this is a new discipline. Psychologists have only paid really intensive and serious attention to this new branch of psychology in the past twenty-five years. Systematic research has only started during that period. Larson et al. [1] surveyed the issues of four major psychiatric journals from a period of five years—from 1978 to 1982—and found that only 2,5% of the quantitative studies included religious and/or spiritual topics.

The first handbook dealing with the psychology of religion and spirituality was published as late as 2005. The volume, edited by Paloutzian and Parks [2], with its 30 chapters written by 45 authors, offers a good insight into the most important conceptual and methodological issues of religion psychology. The chapter dealing with the neuro-psychology of religious and spiritual experience deserves special attention. In this chapter, the interrelation between the cognitive processes and the structures of the brain responsible for the emergence or appearance of religious and spiritual experience are examined. The chapters that analyse the development of religion and spirituality through human life—starting in childhood to old age—discuss the emergence and development of the concept of God in a new approach.

An increasing number of research projects

have been carried out in the past ten or fifteen years in order to reveal the effects of religion and spirituality on people's physical and mental state [3, 4, 5].

As the connection between spirituality and religiouness and health was drawn to the focus of interest of researchers in the middle of 1990s, the "language" of spirituality was also created gradually, it began to develop, and the changes continue today.

Today there are scales—e.g., the Estimation Scale pof Chronicle Illness Therapy, Spiritual Well-Being Scale—that are designed to measure the spiritual well-being and its changes in individuals suffering from certain chronic illnesses during the therapic process, using a religious perspective that is not restrictive, so it is applicable for individuals of different religious backgrounds [6].

Today, the polarization of the two terms is observable: religiousness means everything that is formal, institutional, doctrinal, authoritarian and external, whereas spiritual represents things that are subjective, personal, emotional, internal and not systematic [7].

In Underwood's [8] interpretation, the adjective "religious" refers to a person who is in contact with people who think in a similar way and who share a religion (belief) and belong to a group and practice their religion together. Spirituality, on the other hand, deals with the transcendental and formulates the ultimate questions regarding the purpose of life, with the presupposition that life is more than what we are able to see, hear, perceive or fully comprehend. Spirituality goes beyond the self, and deals with the issues of compassion toward other people. When spirituality appears in a religious context, it may express more than the internal or personal dimension of religious life, it may also include the personal connection with God or the personal habits and practices through which the individual practices compassion. If we extract spirituality from the religious context, the concept becomes so vague that at the extreme end; it looses its meaning. While religion helps to maintain a spiritual life, and spirituality is often an important aspect of the life of religious people, it is possible to use the external features of religion without a closer link to the transcendental.

1.2. Spiritual Consciousness

Spirituality has a number of definitions; Underwood [8] has collected more than 200 from various points of the world.

Moberg [9] believes that spirituality is an internal resource of humans; it is the basic value around which all the other values cluster. It is the central way of looking at things; let the person be religious, anti-religious or non-religious, this is what guides the person's way of life, this is the supernatural, and not the material dimension of human nature. In this interpretation, every person is spiritual, including those who do not attend religious institutions and do not practice religion.

Pargament and Mahonay [10] believe that spirituality is a process, the purpose of which is seeking, finding and maintaining sacred things in human life. This quest takes place in a broader religious context, which can be traditional or one lacking traditionality.

Eckhart Tolle [11, 12] draws our attention to another approach to spirituality. In his opinion, our present consciousness opens up the gate to spirituality. The individual must experience the present moment, while the alertness of his/her consciousness enables the person to view his or her own thoughts, emotions and reactions triggered by the stimuli of the environment. The Presence thus created (conscious alertness) brings about the sense of tranquility and internal peace. The sustained conscious attention launches the spiritual process of transubstatiation that leads the individual to a Spiritual Consciousness, new perspective and new ways of observations. This process, by transforming the consciousness of the person, changes the entire personality of the individual.

Eckhart Tolle [12] asserts that the most important hampering factor in this process is the Ego. It means the conventional, ordinary "self," which constitutes the common mistake in which the illusory belief in the personal identity is rooted. This illusory self will then be the basis of all mental processes, human relations and the interpretation of reality.

The components of the Ego are thoughts, emotions, memories (with which the person identifies as the "history of me"), fixed unconscious roles and collective identifications (nationality, religion, etc.). Most people completely identify with these components of the Ego, and for them no self "outside" this exists. Tolle describes this situation as existence in a "spiritually unconscious" way.

The transformation of the conscience, the beginning of spiritual consciousness, is when the person experiences that he or she is the consciuosness that perceives the operation of Ego.

In Tolle's opinion, when a person is aware that he/she is thinking, the consciousness that experiences this is not part of the person's thinking. This is another dimension of conscience. The spiritual awakening means for the person the ability "to clearly see that what I perceive, experience, think or feel, is after all not the same as what I am." As soon as a person recognizes who he or she is not, immediately comes the recognition of who he or she actually is: "the light of conscience, in which perceptions, experiences, thoughts and emotions come and go. This consciousness in the background, is the deeper, real self." [11, 12].

In order to achieve this consciousness, the person must know him/herself; he or she must get acquainted with the Ego and its functional mechanisms. The Ego is shaped by the past, determining its structure and contents.

The structure of the Ego is an unconscious factor, which forces the individual to reinforce his/her indentity by joining an external object. The content of the Ego will then be the thing with which the individual indentified him/herself (my house, my car, my child, my intelligence, my opinion, etc.).

The contents of the Ego (with which the individual identifies) are shaped by the environment and upbringing of the person, that is, the culture in which the person becomes an adult.

The identification of the Ego with things (object, the person's own body, way of thinking) creates the link of the individual to various things. The Ego (and thus the spiritually unconscious person) experiences his/her existence through the possession of various objects.

The satisfaction provided by the sense of possession is, however, short, so the individual usually carries on the pursuit for new objects.

There is a powerful motivation behind this

activity of the individual, a psychological demand to obtain more, the unconscious sense of "not yet enough," and this feeling surfaces in a want for more.

Tolle believes that this want is a more powerful driving force for the Ego than the desire to possess. The uneasy feelings, recklessness, boredom, stress and dissatisfaction are all largely the products of the dissatisfied longing for more.

The thoughts such as "it's mine," "I want it," "I need it," "it is not enough," belong to the structure of the Ego. The content of the Ego changes with time; it is replaced with new contents. No content is, however, able to lastingly satisfy the Ego as long as the structure of the Ego remains in its place. The invididual keeps looking for something different, something that promises a greater satisfaction, making the sense of self of the individual more complete.

This structure determines the various functions of the Ego. In Tolle's opinion, the most important of the functions are the following:

- The Ego strives to protect, sustain and expand itself,

- The Ego functions in survival mode.

One of the most important strategies of the Ego to sustain and reinforce itself is the experience of "I am right." This is the identification of an idea, position, evaluation. Nothing gives the Ego more power than experiencing that "I am right."

One of the favourite self-reinforcing strategies of the Ego is complaining. Complaining implies the sense that "I am right." When another Ego refuses to accept that "I am right," it is an offence to the complaining Ego, which. in turn, further reinforces its self-awareness.

The statement that the Ego functions in a survival mode means that it continually struggles to remain "psychologically alive," so it regards other Egos as rivals or even enemies. It is the desire of the Ego to be right, and thus overcome the other, ensuring its own superiority.

Tolle believes that the Ego is not bad, it is simply unconscious. If an individual is able to notice and observe the functions of the Ego, he or she will be able to transcend it. In that case, the individual who has been looking for a more complete perception of the self will recognize that it has always been there, but the functions of the Ego—identification with objects and thoughts—has pushed it into the background. One of the ways of transcending the Ego is not reacting wholeheartedly to the ever-changing caleidoscope of thoughts and emotions, but concentrating on the alert consciousness in the background instead.

Only the consciousness of the current moment is able to terminate the illusory self-interpretation and elevate the person's consciousness to a higher, more spiritual level.

Tolle [12] believes that this Spiritual Consciousness has already appeared at a small, but rapidly increasing part of mankind.

1.2. Research Hypotheses

Our initial research hypotheses were the following:

1. The Spiritual Consciousness is now observable among college students

2. There is no difference between the genders in terms of the Spiritual Consciousness

2. Results

2.1. Psychometric Characteristics of the Spiritual Consciousness Scale

As the first step in the compilation of the questionnaire, we defined the construction (Spiritual Consciousness) that we intended to measure with the scale. For an operational definition of the construction, we formulated statements, following the teachings of Eckhart Tolle [11,12].

1. 1 I believe that the continual stream of my thoughts is recurrent and pointless;
2. I am overcome by joy and tranquility without any particular reason;
3. I believe that I am unable to find myself in external things (house, car, money);

4. I think that my thoughts and emotions only constitute a small fragment of what I actually am;
5. I believe that behind the external shape of my body there is an inner vitality, intensively vivid field of energy;
6. I think that the things around me—even the inanimate ones—have a soul;
7. I do not react to my thoughts and emotions, I simply let them happen;
8. I forgive other people because I understand that they are unable to behave in any other way;
9. I think that I am right in many things, but others do not acknowledge that;
10. I get offended easily;
11. In conversations, I mention things that I possess in order to look more valuable in the eyes of others;
12. I feel that nothing is enough for me, I always long for something more, something different;
13. I often think of the future;
14. I feel it a burden having to do what I am doing;

15. I tend to brood on offences that I suffer;
16. I feel apprehension and anger if somebody is more successful than I am;
17. I think I am a special person, standing out of the average;
18. I think that I am reckless and dissatisfied;
19. I tend to complain about other people;
20. I believe that I am the consciousness behind my thoughts and emotions.

This primary scale, consisting of 20 statements (scale: 1=never or almost never, 2= rarely, 3=sometimes, 4= on the majority of days, 5= every day, 6= many times a day), was tested with the help of 400 individuals (200 men, 200 women).

The criteria for selecting the appropriate items were the following:

- Selecting the items characterized by the largest item-surplus correlation;
- The items should be clearcut, easily identifiable ones, thus eliminating items containing redundant elements.

When the scale was finalized, only the most reliable statements were retained, and the ones not matching the criteria above were omitted. In this way, the final number of items was 16.

For the item-surplus correlations, the average values for each items and the dispersion, see Chart 1.

Chart 1. The item-surplus correlations and descriptive statistical figures of the Spiritual Consciousness Scale

Item of New Spiritual Con-sciousness Scale	Item-surplus correlation	Mean Value	Standard Deviation
1. I believe that the continual stream of my thoughts is recurrent and pointless	0,61	2,12	0,91
2. I am overcome by joy and tranquility without any particular reason	0,63	3,20	1,15

3. I believe that I am unable to find myself in external things (house, car, money)	0,54	2,39	1,11
4. I think that my thoughts and emotions only constitute a small fragment of what I actually am	0,51	2,17	1,13
5. I believe that behind the external shape of my body there is an inner vitality, intensively vivid field of energy	0,48	3,65	1,48
6. I think that the things around me—even the inanimate ones—have a soul	0,46	2,93	1,10
7. I do not react to my thoughts and emotions, I	0,56	2,35	1,22

simply let them happen			
8. I think that I am right in many things, but others do not acknowledge that	0,67	4,39	1,07
9. I get offended easily	0,59	3,30	1,21
Item of New Spiritual Consciousness Scale	Item-surplus correlation	Mean Value	Standard Deviation
10, In conversations, I mention things that I possess in order to look more valuable in the eyes of others	0,61	3,94	0,99
11. I feel that nothing is enough for me, I always long for something more, something different	0,68	4,99	1,25
12. I feel it a burden having to do what I	0,45	3,56	1,01

am doing			
13. I tend to brood on offences that I suffer	0,50	3,36	1,21
14. I think that I am reckless and dissatisfied	0,55	3,39	1,17
15. I tend to complain about other people	0,52	3,64	0,98
16. I believe that I am the consciousness behind my thoughts and emotions	0,57	3,09	1,18

The item surplus correlations express the relationship of the items with the totality of the surplus items. The lowest relationship indicator was found at items 12 and 6, and the strongest found at items 8 and 6.

The reliability of the final version of the scale is indicated by the high value of the inner consistency (Cronbach-alfa=0,89). The indicators of internal consistency were similar in both genders.

The reliability of the scale and its particular items for an extended period of time was tested with the help of a group of 140 college students (70 women and 70 men). The reliability of the scale was found to be good again (Chart 2).

Chart 2. Indicators of the reliability of the Spiritual Consciousness Scale over an extended period of time

Item of New Spiritual Consciousness Scale	Test-retest (n=140)
1. I believe that the continual stream of my thoughts is recurrent and pointless	0,83
2. I am overcome by joy and tranquility without any particular reason	0,84
3. I believe that I am unable to find myself in external things (house, car, money)	0,81
4. I think that my thoughts and emotions only constitute a small fragment of what I actually am	0,88
5. I believe that behind the external shape of my body there is an inner vitality, intensively vivid field of energy	0,79
6. I think that the things around me—even the inanimate ones—have a soul	0,80
7. I do not react to my thoughts and emotions, I simply let them happen	0,81
8. I think that I am right in many things, but others do not acknowledge that	0,84
9. I get offended easily	0,81
10, In conversations, I mention things that I possess in order to look more valuable in the eyes of others	0,79
11. I feel that nothing is enough for me, I always long for something more, something different	0,86

12. I feel it a burden having to do what I am doing	0,87
13. I tend to brood on offences that I suffer	0,81
14. I think that I am reckless and dissatisfied	0,82
15. I tend to complain about other people	0,85
16. I believe that I am the consciousness behind my thoughts and emotions	0,80

The factor structure of the questionnaire was also examined, with the results summed up in Chart 3.

Chart 3. The factor structure of Spiritual Consciousness Scale

Item of New Spiritual Consciousness Scale	Factors		
	1	2	3
I think that I am right in many things, but others do not acknowledge that	-,431		
I get offended easily	-,447		
In conversations, I mention things that I possess in order to look more valuable in the eyes of others	-,508		
I feel that nothing is enough for me, I always long for something more, something different	-,640		
I feel it a burden having to do what I am doing	-,611		
I tend to brood on offences that I suffer	-,576		
I think that I am reckless	-,662		

and dissatisfied			
I tend to complain about other people	-,669		
I am overcome by joy and tranquility without any particular reason		,705	
I believe that behind the external shape of my bo-dy there is an inner vitality, intensively vivid field of energy		,667	
I think that the things around me—even the inanimate ones—have a soul		,631	
I believe that I am the consciousness behind my thoughts and emotions		,510	
I believe that the continual stream of my thoughts is recurrent and pointless			,518
I believe that I am unable to find myself in external things (house, car, money)			,698
I think that my thoughts and emotions only constitute a small fragment of what I actually am			,488
I do not react to my thoughts and emotions, I simply let them happen			,654

The criterion of the applicability of the factor analysis is that the data items should be in interrelation with each other, and the variables should contain redundant information.

The strength of the interrelations was indicated by the Kaiser-Meyer-Olkin (KMO) value. The KMO value was in our case 0,728, which indicates the applicability of the variables for a factor analysis.

As a result of the factor analysis, the statements on the scale were arranged into three factors, explaining 62,2% of the variance.

The first factor (eigenvalue: 3.79) explained 24,5 percent of the complete variance. The following items of the Spiritual Consciousness Scale belonged to this factor:

- I think that I am right in many things, but others do not acknowledge that
- I get offended easily
- In conversations, I mention things that I possess in order to look more valuable in the eyes of others
- I feel that nothing is enough for me, I always long for something more, something different

- I feel it a burden having to do what I am doing
- I tend to brood on offences that I suffer
- I think that I am reckless and dissatisfied
- I tend to complain about other people

The statements belonging to this factor contain the excessive activity of the Ego and its reactive answers to the environment. The results of the factor analysis indicate a fall in the activity of this Ego, a reduction in its reactivity. We, therefore, named this factor *"Ego-dyastole"* sub-scale.

The second factor (eigenvalue: 2.714) explained 20,3 percent of the total variance. The following items of the Spiritual Consciousness Scale belonged to this factor:

- I am overcome by joy and tranquility without any particular reason
- I believe that behind the external shape of my body there is an inner vitality, intensively vivid field of energy
- I think that the things around me—even the inanimate ones—have a soul
- I believe that I am the consciousness behind my thoughts and emotions

The statements belonging to this factor refer to experiencing the present in an alert consciousness, so we named this sub-scale

"Alert Consciousness in the Present."

The third factor (eigenvalue: 2.119) explained the 17,4 percent of the total variance. The following items of the Spiritual Consciousness Scale belonged to this factor:

- I believe that the continual stream of my thoughts is recurrent and pointless
- I believe that I am unable to find myself in external things (house, car, money)
- I think that my thoughts and emotions only constitute a small fragment of what I actually am
- I do not react to my thoughts and emotions, I simply let them happen

The statements belonging to this factor indicate that the individual is detached from his/her emotions, own thoughts and the external world, so we called this factor ***"Transcending the functions of Ego"*** sub-scale.

2.2. Participants

We measured the prevelence of Spiritual Consciousness among college students.
Data was collected among students at the

College of Nyíregyháza.

We collected data randomly at every faculty, and participation was voluntary and done with their consent.

Nine hundred students took part in the research, and 854 of them provided valuable data (552 women and 302 men).

The average age was 20,23 (standard deviation 1,51) the median value was 20 years.

2.3. Measures

2.3.1. Examination of Spiritual Consciousness
Spiritual Consciousness Scale

2.4. Comparative Statistics

The proportion of answers (%) given to the items of the "Ego-dyastole" sub-scale of the Spiritual Consciousness Scale are summed up in Chart 4.

Chart 4. The proportion of answers (%) given to the items of the "Ego-dyastole" sub-scale of the Spiritual Consciousness Scale

Item of Ego-dyastole sub-scale	1	2	3	4	5	6
1. I think that I am right in many things, but others do not acknowledge that	3,3	5,2	21,5	38,6	27,5	3,9
2. I get offended easily	2,6	6,5	12,5	30,1	33,3	15,6
3. In conversations, I mention things that I possess in order to look more valuable in the eyes of others	0,7	2,1	7,8	17	39,8	32,6
4. I feel that nothing is enough for me, I always long for something more, something different	3,3	9,8	20,9	24,8	32,7	8,5
5. I feel it a burden having	2	1,3	8,5	29,5	45	13,7

to do what I am doing						
6. I tend to brood on offences that I suffer	2,6	5,2	13,7	26,8	35,4	16,3
7. I think that I am reckless and dissatisfied	1,3	7,8	8,6	32	34	16,3
8. I tend to complain about other people	1,3	2,6	5,9	26,2	49	15

1=never or almost never, 2= rarely, 3=sometimes, 4= on the majority of days, 5= every day, 6= many times a day.

The items of the "Ego-dyastole" sub-scale indicate a reduction in the operation of the Ego so students with a Spiritual Consciousness tended to score low at this sub-scale, as they answered that they never, very rarely or rarely experienced the behaviour patterns there described.

Item 1 of the "Ego-dyastole" sub-scale:

- I think that I am right in many things, but others do not acknowledge that

Of the college students, 70% experience this emotion every day or a majority of the days, whereas 30% of them never, very rarely or rarely do.

Item 2 of the "Ego-dyastole" sub-scale:

- I get offended easily

Of the college students, 79% behave that way every day or a majority of the days, whereas 21% of them never, very rarely or rarely do.

Item 3 of the "Ego-dyastole" sub-scale:

- In conversations, I mention things that I possess in order to look more valuable in the eyes of others

Of the college students, 89,4% behave that way every day or a majority of the days, whereas 10,6% of them never, very rarely or rarely do.

Item 4 of the "Ego-dyastole" sub-scale:

- I feel that nothing is enough for me, I always long for something more, something different

Of the college students, 66% experience this emotion every day or a majority of the days, whereas 34% of them never, very rarely or rarely do.

Item 5 of the "Ego-dyastole" sub-scale:

- I feel it a burden having to do what I am doing

Of the college students, 88,2% behave that way every day or a majority of the days, whereas 11,8% of them never, very rarely or rarely do.

Item 6 of the "Ego-dyastole" sub-scale:

- I tend to brood on offences that I suffer

Of the college students, 78,5% behave that way every day or a majority of the days, whereas 21,5% of them never, very rarely or rarely do.

Item 7 of the "Ego-dyastole" sub-scale:

- I think that I am reckless and dissatisfied

Of the college students, 82,3% experience this emotion every day or a majority of the days, whereas 17,7% of them never, very rarely or rarely do.

Item 8 of the "Ego-dyastole" sub-scale:

- I tend to complain about other people

Of the college students, 90,2% behave that way every day or a majority of the days, whereas 9,8% of them never, very rarely or rarely do.

The proportion of answers (%) given to the items of the "Alert Consciousness in the Present" sub-scale of the Spiritual Consciousness Scale are summed up in Chart 5.

Chart 5. The proportion of answers (%) given to the items of the "Alert Consciousness in the Present" sub-scale of the Spiritual Consciousness Scale

Item of "Alert Consciousness in the Present" sub-scale	1	2	3	4	5	6
1. I am overcome by joy and tranquility without any particular reason	6,5	18,4	39,3	25,6	5,9	3,3
2. I believe that behind the external shape of my	8,5	15,7	19,6	28,7	13,1	14,4

body there is an inner vitality, intensively vivid field of energy						
3. I think that the things around me— even the inanimate ones—have a soul	23,5	18,9	26,8	11,9	9,1	9,8
4. I believe that I am the consciousness behind my thoughts and emotions	9,8	17	37,2	22,9	8,5	4,6

1=never or almost never, 2= rarely, 3=sometimes, 4= on the majority of days, 5= every day, 6= many times a day.

The items of the "Alert Consciousness at Present" sub-scale indicate the alert consciousness of "here and now," so students at a higher grade of Spiritual Consciousness scored higher at this sub-scale. They experience the emotions described in the statements every day or on the majority of the days.

Item 1 of the "Alert Consciousness in the Present" sub-scale:

- I am overcome by joy and tranquility without any particular reason

Of the college students, 34,8% of them experience this emotion every day or a majority of the days, whereas 65,2% of them never, very rarely or rarely do.

Item 2 of the "Alert Consciousness in the Present" sub-scale:

- I believe that behind the external shape of my body there is an inner vitality, intensively vivid field of energy

Of the college students, 56,2% of them experience this emotion every day or a majority of the days, whereas 43,8% of them never, very rarely or rarely do.

Item 3 of the "Alert Consciousness in the Present" sub-scale:

- I think that the things around me—even the inanimate ones—have a soul

Of the college students, 30,8% of them experience this emotion every day or a majority of the days, whereas 69,2% of them never, very rarely or rarely do.

Item 4 of the "Alert Consciousness in the Present" sub-scale:

- I believe that I am the consciousness behind my thoughts and emotions

Of the college students, 36% experience this emotion every day or a majority of the days, whereas 64% of them never, very rarely or rarely do.

The proportion of answers (%) given to the items of the "Transcending the functions of Ego" sub-scale of the Spiritual Consciousness Scale are summed up in Chart 6.

Chart 6. The proportion of answers (%) given to the items of the "Transcending the functions of Ego" sub-scale of the Spiritual Consciousness Scale

Item of "Transcending the functions of Ego" sub-scale	1	2	3	4	5	6
1. I believe that the continual stream of my thoughts is recurrent and pointless	27,4	37,7	31,4	2,1	0,7	0,7
2. I believe that I am unable to find myself in external things (house, car, money)	24,2	33,3	26,8	11,8	3,2	0,7
3. I think that my thoughts and emotions only constitute a small fragment of what I actually am	35,9	26,8	25,5	8,5	2,6	0,7
4. I do not react to my thoughts and emotions, I simply let them happen	27,5	34,7	21,7	9,8	3,3	2

1=never or almost never, 2= rarely, 3=sometimes, 4= on the majority of days, 5= every day, 6= many times a day.

The items of the sub-scale called "Transcending the functions of Ego" indicate that the individual is detached from his/her emotions, own thoughts and the external world, so students at a higher grade of Spiritual Consciousness scored higher at this sub-scale.

They experience the emotions and show the behaviour patterns described in the statements every day or on the majority of the days.

Item 1 of the "Transcending the functions of Ego" sub-scale:

- I believe that the continual stream of my thoughts is recurrent and pointless

Of the college students, 3,5% of them experience this emotion every day or a majority of the days, whereas 96,5% of them never, very rarely or rarely do.

Item 2 of the "Transcending the functions of Ego" sub-scale:

- I believe that I am unable to find myself in external things (house, car, money)

Of the college students, 15,7% of them experience this emotion every day or a majority of the days, whereas 84,3% of them never, very rarely or rarely do.

Item 3 of the "Transcending the functions of Ego" sub-scale:

- I think that my thoughts and emotions only constitute a small fragment of what I actually am

Of the college students, 11,8% of them experience this emotion every day or a majority of the days, whereas 88,2% of them never, very rarely or rarely do.

Item 4 of the "Transcending the functions of Ego" sub-scale:
- I do not react to my thoughts and emotions, I simply let them happen

Of the college students, 15,1% of them behave that way every day or a majority of the days, whereas 84,9% of them never, very rarely or rarely do.

Chart 7 contains the descriptive and comparative statistics of the results of the

Spiritual Consciousness Scale.

Chart 7. The descriptive and comparative statistics of the results of the Spiritual Consciousness Scale

	Total (n=854)		Women (n=552)		Men (n=302)	
	Mean Value	Standard De-viation	Mean Value	Standard De-viation	Mean Value	Standard De-viation
Sub-scale of New Spirit ual Cons cious ness Scale	55,9	6,6	55,8	6,3	55,4	8,1
"Ego-dyast ole" sub-scale	34,2	5,8	34,2	5,2	34,3	8,2
"Aler t Cons cious ness in the Prese nt" sub-	12,9	3,5	12,9	3,4	12,8	4,3

scale						
"Transcending the functions of Ego"s sub-scale	9,1	2,7	9,2	2,7	8,9	2,7

The chart indicates that there is no difference between men and women at the Spiritual Consciousness Scale and its sub-scales.

We intended to survey the structure of Spiritual Consciousness among college students. In order to make the specific elements of Spiritual Consciousness comparable to each other, we calculated the average of the answers given to the statements on the sub-scales concerned. It is summed up in Chart 8.

Chart 8. The average of the answers given to a statement on the sub-scales of the Spiritual Consciousness Scale

Sub-scale of New Spiritual Consciousnes s Scale	Total (n=854)	Wom-en (n=552)	Men (n=302)
	Mean Value	Mean Value	Mean Value
"Ego-dyastole" sub-scale	4,3	4,3	4,3

"Alert Consciousnes s in the Present" sub-scale	3,2	3,2	3,2
"Transcendin g the functions of Ego" sub-scale	2,3	2,3	2,2

As it is indicated in the figure, the college students—regardless of their genders—tended to achieve the highest values at the "Ego dyastole" sub-scale out of the components of the Spiritual Consciousness, as this was observable in the majority of the students on the majority of days.

It was followed by the sub-scale named Alert Consciousness in the Present," as the majority of the students had experienced it several times. The lowest values were measured in the sub-scale "Transcending the functions of Ego" as the majority of the students had only occassionally experienced the emotions described in the statements of that sub-scale.

3. Conclusion

Following the teachings of Eckhart Tolle, the author created the Spiritual Consciousness Scale (SCS) and carried out its statistical analysis.

The purpose has been developing a new measuring instrument for the recognition of spiritual consciousness. An attempt has been made to find out whether this new consciousness exists at all and to what extent it is present in the population concerned (college students).

The psychometric survey with the Spiritual Consciousness Scale was conducted with a sample of 400 college students. As part of the survey, three dimensions of the Spiritual Consciousness were revealed: "Ego-dyastole" (reduction in the functions of Ego), "Alert consciousness in the present" and "Transcending the functions of Ego."

The measuring instrument thus created was used to seek an answer to the question as to whether the Spiritual Consciousness was present among college students, and whether there was any difference between the two genders in this respect. Eight hundred and fifty-four students were involved in the survey.

Our research has verified our research hypothesis, that is, Spiritual Consciousness is present among college students.

The findings of a research project we had conducted earlier showed that although the majority of college students formally belonged to some religious denomination or community, they were not really religious, not practicing their faith in daily life. It coincides with the general experience that adolescents and young adults tend to be less religious that elderly people [13].

Among college students, the "Alert consciousness in the present" dimension of the Spiritual Consciousness had the highest prevalence. Within that dimension, the sense of an "inner body" (an internal vividness behind the external body) was the most common. Of the students, 14,4% experience this feeling several times a day and 13,1% of them at least once a day. An individual is only able to experience this emotion if he or she is consciously experiencing the current moment.

Of the college students, 9,8% experiences an emotion several times a day and 9,1% does so once a day that the surrounding world is the reflection of the universal existence. Of the students, 8,5% see themselves in moments of clear conscience several times a day and 4,6% of them experiences this at least once a day. Of the students, 5,9% experience the sense of peace and happiness without any particular reason every day, and 3,3% of them are visited by this feeling several times a day.

The second most common dimension of Spiritual Consciousness was "Ego-dyastole." Within that, the reduction of the desire to possess things was particularly conspicuous.

Of the students, 9,8% rarely and 3,3% of them never or almost never experienced the longing for something more. Being offended and nursing, sustaining the sense of being offended as the strategies of reinforcing the Ego also had a diminishing tendency among many of the college students (rarely: 6,5%, never or almost never 2,6%; nursing the sense of being offended: rarely 5,2%, never or almost never 2,6%). The prevalence of experiencing the sense of "I am right" as a strategy of sustaining and reinforcing the Ego also diminished considerably among college students. Of those college students, 5,2% of them rarely and 3,3% of them never or almost never experience this emotion. Of the college students, 7,8% rarely experience the recklessness and dissatisfaction rooted in dissatisfied want and desires, and 1,3% of them almost never do. The withdrawal of the Ego was the least spectacular at complaining (rarely 2,6%, never or almost never 1,3% of them complain) and boasting (2,1% boast rarely, 0,7% never or almost never do so).

The prevalence of "Transcending the functions of Ego" was the least common among the components of the Spiritual Consciousness.

Within that dimension, transcending thinking and emotions were the most frequent patterns of behaviour. 3,3% of the students experience this impression daily and 2% several times a day. Of the students, 2,6% have the impression that their thoughts and emotions constitute only a small fragment of their real personalities, and 0,7% of them encounter this feeling several times a day. In the frequency of occurence, this was followed by the detachment from external things, which was experienxced by 3,2% of the students every day and 0,7% of them several times a day. Students appeared to be least capable of transcending the perpetual operation of thinking; only 1,4% of them experienced that the stream of their was aimless and repetitive.

It was also possible to verify our second hypothesis, in which we assumed that there were no major differences in the prevalence of Spiritual Consciousness between the two genders.

Examining everyday spirituality, David et al. [14] found that women were characterized by spirituality to a considerably larger extent than men. Women scored significantly higher in categories of religiousness and spirituality such as private religious practice, beliefs, forgiveness, religious/spiritual coping, religious commitment and institutional-organizational religious practice.

Tolle [12] argues that the emergence of the Spiritual Consciousness is relatively independent of gender; it appears in men as well as in women. Our research findings underpin this opinion, as we were unable to reveal any considerable difference between the genders in any of the dimensions of Spiritual Consciousness.

Spiritual Consciousness Scale

Please, read all statements carefully and mark the alternative that best describes your emotions and behaviour by the number of each statement on the answer sheet, according to the following criteria:

SCALE: 1=never or almost never, 2=rarely, 3=sometimes, 4=on the majority of days, 5=every day, 6=many times a day

Before submitting the sheet, please check whether you have answered all the statements.

	1	2	3	4	5	6
1. I believe that the continual stream of my thoughts is recurrent and pointless						
2. I am overcome by joy and tranquility without any particular reason						
3. I believe that I am unable to find myself in						

external things (house, car, money)					
4. I think that my thoughts and emotions only constitute a small fragment of what I actually am	1	2	3	4	5	6
5. I believe that behind the external shape of my body there is an inner vitality, intensively vivid field of energy	1	2	3	4	5	6
6. I think that the things around me—even the inanimate ones—have a soul	1	2	3	4	5	6
7. I do not react to my thoughts and emotions, I simply let them happen	1	2	3	4	5	6
8. I think that I am right in many things, but others do not acknowledge that	1	2	3	4	5	6

	1	2	3	4	5	6
9. I get offended easily	1	2	3	4	5	6
10, In conversations, I mention things that I possess in order to look more valuable in the eyes of others	1	2	3	4	5	6
11. I feel that nothing is enough for me, I always long for something more, something different	1	2	3	4	5	6
12. I feel it a burden having to do what I am doing	1	2	3	4	5	6
13. I tend to brood on offences that I suffer	1	2	3	4	5	6
14. I think that I am reckless and dissatisfied	1	2	3	4	5	6
15. I tend to complain about other people	1	2	3	4	5	6
16. I believe that I am the consciousness behind my thoughts and	1	2	3	4	5	6

emotions						

Please give your age, gender, occupation.

Age...

....

Gender...

....

Occupation..

Use of Spiritual Consciousness Scale

*Completing the Questionnaire
and the Process of Assessment*

The questionnaire for self-description may be used for individual and group surveys as well.

In order to provide the respondents with appropriate circumstances for completing the questionnaire, it is advisable to choose a noise-free and well lit room.

If a respondent has difficulties in reading the questionnaire (dyslexia), the person conducting the survey may read the questions out loud and note the answers of the respondent.

Instructions on the Questionnaire

Please, read all statements carefully and mark the alternative that best describes your emotions and behaviour by the number of each statement on the answer sheet, according to the following criteria:

SCALE: 1=never or almost never, 2=rarely, 3=sometimes, 4=on the majority of days, 5=every day, 6=many times a day

Before submitting the sheet, please check whether you have answered all the statements.

Our preliminary experience suggests that the average college student will need approximately ten to fifteen minutes to complete the questionnaire.

The first step in the manual assessment of the questionnaire is summing up the points given to the items that make up the dimensions.

The items belonging to the specific dimensions are shown in Chart 1

Chart 1. The items that belong to the specific dimensions of Spiritual Consciousness Scale

Sub-scale of Spiritual Consciousness Scale	Items
"Ego-dyastole" sub-scale	8, 9, 10, 11, 12, 13, 14, 15
"Alert Consciousness in the Present" sub-scale	2, 5, 6, 16
"Transcending the functions of Ego" sub-scale	1, 3, 4, 7

In the dimensions "Alert consciousness in the present" and "Transcending the functions of Ego" of Spiritual Consciousness Scale, the assessment is done in the following way:

Never or almost never (1), Rarely (2), Sometimes (3), On the majority of days (4), Every day (5), Many times a day (6)

In the case of the "Ego-dyastole" sub-scale, the system of grading is reversed, so it is done according to the following scale:

Never or almost never (6), Rarely (5), Sometimes (4), On the majority of days (3), Every day (2), Many times a day (1)

The indicator of Spiritual Consciousness is the summary of the points given to the sub-scales of the Spiritual Consciousness Scale (Chart 2).

Chart 2. The points that belong to the items of the Spiritual Consciousness Scale

1. I believe that the continual stream of my thoughts is recurrent and pointless	1	2	3	4	5	6
2. I am overcome by joy and tranquility without any particular reason	1	2	3	4	5	6
3. I believe that I am unable to find myself in external things (house, car, money)	1	2	3	4	5	6
4. I think that my thoughts and emotions only constitute a small fragment of what I actually am	1	2	3	4	5	6
5. I believe that behind the external shape of my	1	2	3	4	5	6

body there is an inner vitality, intensively vivid field of energy						
6. I think that the things around me—even the inanimate ones—have a soul	1	2	3	4	5	6
7. I do not react to my thoughts and emotions, I simply let them happen	1	2	3	4	5	6
8. I think that I am right in many things, but others do not acknowledge that	6	5	4	3	2	1
9. I get offended easily	6	5	4	3	2	1
10.In conversations, I mention things that I possess in order to look more valuable in the eyes of	6	5	4	3	2	1

others					
11. I feel that nothing is enough for me, I always long for something more, something different	6	5	4	3	2	1
12. I feel it a burden having to do what I am doing	6	5	4	3	2	1
13. I tend to brood on offences that I suffer	6	5	4	3	2	1
14. I think that I am reckless and dissatisfied	6	5	4	3	2	1
15. I tend to complain about other people	6	5	4	3	2	1
16. I believe that I am the consciousness behind my thoughts and emotions	1	2	3	4	5	6

It is possible to well use the questionnaire for research.

References

[1]   Larson, D.B., & Pattison, E.M., & Blazer,
       D.G., & Omran, A.R., & Kaplan, B.H.
       (1986): Systematic analysis of research on
       religious variables in four major psychiatric
       journals, 1978-1982. *American Journal of
       Psychiatry,* 143, 329-334

[2]   Paloutzian, R.F., & Park, C.L. (Eds.) (2005):
       *Handbook of the Psychology of Religion and
       Spirituality.* The Guilford Press, New York.

[3]   Levin, J.S., & Chatters, L.M., & Taylor, R.J.
       (1995): Religious effects on health status and
       religious behaviour. *J. Gerontol: Soc Sci,.* 50:
       154-163.

[4]   George, L.K., & Ellison, C.G., & Larson,
       D.B. (2002): Exploring the relationships
       between religious involvement and health.
       Psychological Inquiry, 3: 190-200,

[5]   Powell, L.H., & Shababi, L., & Thoresen,
       C.E. (2003): Religion and spirituality:
       Linkages to physical health. *American
       Psychologyst,* 58: 36-52.

[6]   Peterman, A.H., & Fitchett, G., & Brady,
       M.J., & Hernandez, L., & Cella, D. (2002):
       Measuring spiritual well-being in people with
       cancer: the Functional Assessment of
       Chronic Illness Therapy-Spiritual Well-Being

Scale (Facit-Sp). *Annals of Behavioral Medicine*, 24:1, 49.

[7] Koenig, H.G., & McCullough, M.E., & Larson, D.B. (2001): *Handbook of religion and health.* New York, Oxford University Press.

[8] Underwood, L.G. (2006): Ordinary spiritual experience: Qualitative research, interpretive guidelines, and population distribution for the daily spiritual experience scale. *Archive for the Psychology of Religion*, 28: 181-218.

[9] Moberg, D.O. (1984): Subjective measures of spiritual well-being. *Review of Religious Research*, 25:4, 351-359.

[10] Pargament, K.I., & Mahoney, A. (2002): Spirituality: The discovery and conservation of the sacred. In: Snyder, C.R., & Lopez, S.J. (Eds.), *Handbook of positive psychology.* New York, Oxford University Press. 646-659.

[11] Tolle, E. (1997): *The Power of Now.* New Wordl Library, Novato.

[12] Tolle, E. (2006): *Új föld [New Earth].* Agykontroll Kft., Budapest.

[13] Beit-Hallahmi, B., & Argyle, M. (1997): *The psychology of religius behaviour, belief and experience.* Routledge, London.

[14] David, J.A., & Smith, T.W., & Marsden, P.V. (2001): *General Social Surveys, 1972-2000 Cumulative Codebook.* Chicago: National Opinion Research Center.